MW00512147

THE COURTS OF HEAVEN

The Courts of Heaven

How to Present Your Case

BILL VINCENT

RWG Publishing

Contents

RWG Publishing
PO Box 596
Litchfield, IL 62056
https://rwgpublishing.com/
Published in the United States of America

Paperback: 978-1-79476-119-3

Chapter 1

The Courts of Heaven:How to Present Your Case

After several books on the courts of heaven and I am thrilled about the results I'm seeing in people's lives, and the testimonies I'm hearing, and you're going to see why I'm happy in Luke chapter 18. And we're going to begin on presenting our cases in the courts of heaven. In Luke, chapter 18, verses 1 through 8, and you may want to underline this. There are several significant thoughts in this passage of Scripture that you'll want to refer to from time to time.

And the Bible says: *"Then Jesus told his disciples a parable, to show them that they should always pray and not give up."* One Version says, *"men ought always to pray, and not give up."* He said, in a particular town, there was a judge who neither feared God nor cared what people thought. There was a widow in that town who kept coming to him with the plea, 'grant me justice against my adversary.' For some time, he refused. But finally, he said to himself, even though I do not fear God, nor do I care what people think yet because this widow keeps bothering me, I will see that she gets justice so that she won't eventually come and attack me. The Lord said, Listen to what the unjust judge says, and will God not bring about justice for his chosen ones who cry out to him day and night? Will he keep putting them off?

I tell you, he will see that they get justice, and quickly. However, when the Son of Man comes, will He find faith on the earth? Now, we want to learn how to present our petitions and our cases before the Lord. See, I want you to step into this dimension and see God's passion toward you. I want you today to purpose in your heart, to begin to move with boldness, to begin to move with confidence before the Lord, before the courts of heaven. First, let me say to most of us, that if there's anything we need to do, we need to get off the battlefield. The first thing we must do is to step into the courts of heaven, and the first thing we need to do to get into the courts of heaven is to get off the battlefield.

You can't be on the battlefield and in the courts of heaven at the same time. We have to recognize the need for legal precedents to be set first before we run out onto the battlefield. We conflict, but before it's a battle, it's a legal conflict. See, I think that the church has put such an emphasis on the battlefield. We're in a war that we forgot that our greatest battle is in the heavenly, not on a battlefield. I want you to know, Jesus never pictured prayer in a battlefield context.

He did, however, put it in a courtroom and a judicial setting, as we saw here in Luke 18, verses 1 through 8. In this parable, the widow is seeking a verdict of justice from a judge – an unrighteous judge. Among other things, one glaring aspect of the story stands out to me, this woman, in her efforts to deal with her adversary, she never spoke to her adversary once but only to the judge. I'm concerned about how many Christians are running around talking to devils. She understood that when a rendering could be obtained from the judge, then her adversary became of no consequence. The adversary's legal footing for hurting, harming, stealing, or tormenting her would be removed. The adversary would have to bend his knee to the verdict of the court.

Once the court rendered a verdict, then it could be executed into place. The verdict from the court is our legal wrestling. We wrestle not against flesh and blood. We wrestle in a court of law, and putting it into place is the battlefield. See, we've tried to run out to the battlefield without verdicts from the court, so we found ourselves ineffective or even soundly defeated. Those days are over as we get off the battlefield, and we get into the courtroom.

So, this is what the Apostle Paul was referring to in Ephesians 6 and verse 12, when he said, *"For we wrestle not against flesh and blood, but against principalities, against powers, against the rulers of darkness of this world, against spiritual hosts of wickedness in heavenly places."* Now, you're going to find out that in those categories, there's seven of them throughout the Scriptures, speaking about different domains that God will lead you into. We found out that there are seven different courtrooms in heaven. Not all of us can go into every courtroom, at least, not all the time. But God will lead you into different courtrooms.

Four of these courtrooms are open to everybody: concerning yourself, concerning your family, concerning areas where he's given you authority over. Then some are being given authority, different levels of authority, and different responsibilities on behalf of the nation. I don't think it's peculiar that there are so many people in this church that are somehow getting involved in politics, some form of social justice. But you have to understand that you will not win those battles just because you have an idea. Those battles must be won in the courts of heaven before you ever obtain them on the battlefield, or in the marketplace. Some of you are going to be Daniels, Josephs, Esthers,

Deborahs, in the marketplace, but you have to go into your spiritual place in the courts to obtain the things God wants you to have in this world, the big deal that's coming.

I'll tell you, I've watched so many people come to me and they think because they can get in front of a minister, just because they can align the pocket of somebody, that they're going to get the deal. Let me tell you something; these are not natural battles you're fighting, they're spiritual battles. These spiritual battles must be fought in a spiritual realm, and you must get a verdict from heaven to enforce it on Earth. If you obtain something and you do not have the legal right to it, you'll have it for a while, but it will be taken from you because, legally, the enemy will come and say he wants to have it. That's why so many prosper for a moment, and then just at the right time; the enemy pulls it all away from you because you didn't obtain it legally.

You know, this idea of wrestling is a very apt term for what goes on in the courts of the Lord. You see, through our maneuvering in the courts, we put into place the necessary legalities for God's kingdom and His will to be done. I don't know if you've ever been in a natural court setting, but even if you go there, you'll attest to it. You'll see that this is what happens in a natural court setting.

Now, it takes some legal wrangling to get this in place. Once it's done, once you have the legal mandate, the verdict, you can march on to your battlefield and win every single time. See, the battle in the courtroom always precedes the victory on the battlefield. Let me say that again. The battle in the courtroom always precedes the victory on the battlefield. See, we are all learning to win in the courtroom so that we can win on the battlefield. Once we can change our perspective, once we can see things differently, and see that the primary place of conflict is in the courtroom, then we'll be ready to present our case. So, today, I'm going to give you some points on how to present your case.

First of all, presenting our case. Well, we can only present our case once we have read from the books of heaven. I'm always shocked at how many people suck stuff out of the air. You're going to approach demons, and you're going to approach Almighty God is what you think. I don't think that's a good idea. He says, *"My word never returns void. It always accomplishes the purposes wherein do I send it."* He says, *"My thoughts are not your thoughts. My ways are not your ways."*

I wouldn't go before God with my ideas. I'd go to God with his ideas. You probably get a better success rate if you honor him with his ideas. Daniel chapter 7 verse 10 sets the scene; it says: *"A fiery stream issued and came forth from before him. 1000 thousand ministered to him; 10,000 times 10,000 stood before him. The court was seated, and the books were opened."*

I tell you what a picture — thousands and thousands of angels, a cloud of witnesses, thousands before him. The books are open. The court is seated. I tell you what, here's the good news: the books are open. The books aren't locked, they're not sealed, and they're not closed. This means that you and I have a right to look into those books. We can discern, by revelation, what are in those books. On a personal level, those books reveal our kingdom purpose, and they reveal our destiny. You know, so many people say, "Yes, I know what I'm supposed to do." I wish I knew what I was supposed to do.

I know part of my purpose. But each time I go before God, it's like, oh, there's another look into what God has for me. Little by little, line upon line, precept upon precept, here a little, there a little, God begins to build you up from grace to grace, from faith to faith, from strength to strength, from revelation to revelation. He doesn't give it to you all at once. He gives it to you as you go and you open the books, you look in, and he'll give you another glimpse, and he'll say, now, take this ground. I promise you, if God had shown me what I would be doing today when I started, I would never have started. Think about it.

See, we have to understand that it's not a once-off revelation, but it's a journey of discovery. When you're dealing with cities or states or nations, let me tell you something, that's where we need legitimate prophecy. Legitimate prophets to help us understand

God's kingdom and His Will as it's written in the books. You know, when a prophet prophesies, he's not telling you your phone number. He should be prophesying what is in the books of heaven, about your future, about a nation. There's an unveiling of secrets contained in these books. A prophet is just reading out of the books of heaven and declaring what he sees.

Once this is done, then you have apostles. Apostles have jurisdiction in a given sphere. They can begin to present cases in the courtrooms of heaven on behalf of nations, churches, and businesses. That's why you have Apostolic cover. That's why you want prophets and apostles. It's not some weird flaky thing you run around, and it's not done on Earth. It's not about oil on Earth, but it's about victories in heaven. We go before God, and we begin to present a city, the state, or the nation in the court. We begin to remind God what was written in the books, and about what he said. We present our case and put God into remembrance.

Isaiah said it this way: *"God said, review the past for me. Let us argue the matter together. State your case for your innocence."* Man, I love that verse. State your case, argue your matter, come before me, and wrestle with me. Make your case so that I can bless you. God is not angry at you. He wants to give you the case you present. You see, this operation sets the court in motion. Just visualize with me, just let your mind run a little bit. Just as in a natural court, the proceeding starts. Now, think about this. The judge on the throne - Almighty God, His son seated next to him, and your advocate. Sometimes, he may be standing next to Jesus, while sometimes, it's the Holy Spirit who's your advocate.

There's a courtroom full of witnesses where a great crowd of witnesses surrounds you. Saints that have gone on before you, angels are witnessing this. And as you stand before the throne, just as in a natural court, the proceeding starts with the prosecution presenting its case. That's a powerful thought that you and I, as mortal people, have the authority to set in motion the courts of heaven. You and I can set the court of heaven in motion. It's true. We begin to present what has been written from the beginning of the world from the books. The court comes into session.

This is why in Daniel 7, the court is seated, and the books are open. See, the court is going to decide based on what is presented from the heavenly books, the books of heaven by you and by me as individuals, and corporately received. That's why all-night prayer meetings or corporate prayer are so important. What an awesome privilege God has given us. Think about it.

Number two. Once you're in the courtroom, we have to learn how to agree with our accuser. Keep reading this until you get my point here. You present your case; you're prosecuting a case, you're trying to bring to bear the witness of the Bible, the Word of

God. That's a book, that book is also open in heaven.
That's the book God gives us to study that unlocks all
the other books through the revelation of His word.
He is the word, and every word that he's written will
never contradict His Word. But once we have presented the case of what has been written in the
books, then we have to understand that we will also
encounter the accuser, seeking to deny us in those
books.

Revelations 12 verse 10 says, *"Then I heard a loud
voice in heaven say, now have come to salvation and
the power and the kingdom of our God and the authority of his Messiah. For the accuser of our brothers
and sisters, who accuses them before our God, day and
night has been hurled down."* See, all accusations he
brings to disqualify us from getting what is in the
books has to be answered. This will require us not to
argue with him but to repent and humble ourselves
before the Lord. We humble ourselves for the Lord, for
nations, and ourselves. It is in the interest of the kingdom that we do so.

In that parable in Luke 18 that we just read, it's
very interesting to me that in the next part, after verse
8, verses 9 through 14, he gives a teaching about two
men that went up to the temple to pray. And he con-
trasts how the Pharisees, who were self-righteous and
arrogant, prayed, and while the tax collector was very
humble and surrendered. The end of the parable was
that the tax collector out of the house of God was

justified, and the Pharisee was not justified. Look at what it says. It says, *"To some who trusted in themselves that they were righteous and despised others."* He was speaking to these people. *"Two men went up to the temple to pray, one a Pharisee and the other a tax collector. The Pharisee didn't pray, thus was himself."*

God, I thank you that I am not like other men, extortioners, unjust, adulterers, or even as this tax collector. I fast, I give tithes of all that I possess. And the tax collector standing afar off would not even so much as raise his eyes to heaven, but beat his breath, saying God be merciful to me a sinner. I tell you, this man went down to his house justified rather than the other. For everyone exalts himself will be humbled, and whoever humbles himself will be exalted.

There's an attitude we need when we go into the courts of heaven. Jesus spoke this parable as a connection to, or at least, as an extension to his teaching of the judicial place. The woman who had importuned. See, to be justified means to be rendered as just or innocent. To be justified is a legal position of being found 'not guilty' or innocent. One of the things that Jesus is teaching in connection to the operation in the courts of heaven is that God responds to humility and surrender.

There's something about surrendering that says, God; you know what, I don't want to get in this place where I think I deserve something. I command heaven. You know, I've learned something, that there are times I even know that I'm right, but I would rather not make the demand but instead say, "Lord, I fall into the merciful hands of God, give me not what I deserve, not what I'm right about, but what do you deserve? What do you think I deserve? I'll surrender myself to your best interest. What would you do for me, Lord?" Because God always does more than I would ever do for myself. And he always has.

Humility, surrender. They carry significant weight in the courts of heaven. If we want to have an audience in the courts, we must appear there with a humble spirit and a broken and contrite heart. These are the sacrifices that God will not despise. Psalm 51 verse 17, *"My sacrifice, oh God, is a broken spirit. A broken and contrite heart, you will not despise."* You see, through repentance, we set in place, the voice of the blood of Jesus and we release every other voice that has a testimony.

Some voices have a testimony: the blood, the name, the Word of God. There is a multitude of voices that we could talk about. You can study it on your own. But these voices can speak into the court system as well. And we can agree with these voices in several ways. One of the primary ways is through our repentance. When we sense accusations being used against us, the accuser or the brethren is constantly accusing you, and we should agree with it.

In Matthew 5 verse 25, it says, Agree with your adversary quickly while you're on the way with him, lest your adversary delivers you to the judge, and the judge hands you over to the officer, and you'll be thrown into prison. Sometimes, you get in the court of heaven, and I want you to know something, you get broadsided. You didn't know that the enemy had that against you. It's no use fighting him. Yeah, but yeah, 'yeah, but' doesn't work in heaven. Just 'Yes, Lord, he's right. I repent. I bring it under the blood of Jesus. I humble myself, and that accusation now becomes a fire through the blood of Jesus. Amen.'

You see, to agree with your adversary means that you're quick to repent of anything being used against us in the court of heaven. I do not need to answer for myself. I don't justify myself for any reason. I allow the blood of Jesus to justify me. Then I can also draw from any other, or all of the other voices in the court that would want to speak as well. Even our cloud of witnesses could speak. It's incredible what goes on in that courtroom, and we're only learning about it now. So, let's ask God to keep showing us, but they will speak on my behalf only as I have repented and have taken access to the blood of Jesus.

You see, self-justification can destroy us, but repentance will cause us to be accepted. We need to repent of anything in our history, or even in our bloodline, those kinds of issues. And we may not even know what they are, but I found that as I get before the Lord, sometimes, he'll bring things to my remembrance. Sometimes, he'll say, do you remember this?

Immediately, I don't let it become an accusation. I just confessed that; I say, "Father, I see that. That was a breach of your law, that was a breach of your word, that's contrary to what your Scripture says, that was considered this or that was considered that, according to the law."

As you grow in the law, as you grow in the teaching of the laws, you grow in the understanding of the Word of God. It shows you your sin, not to condemn you, but so that you can confess it, so you can bring it to the courts of heaven and have it washed. You see, as we begin to repair the things that our bloodlines, even though things that we're not aware of, it's not uncommon for either the enemy or the Holy Spirit to begin to attack us in that bloodline. I know this; there been times I've been moved to sorrow, I've been moved to near tears, a conviction in my heart, the sorrow for the sin that I had allowed or didn't even know was there because the repentance was so real. But when we do that, it takes away the accusation of the devil, and it silences his ability to disqualify us.

Number three, we need to learn how to confess our sins. See, our words before the throne of God are very powerful. In Hosea 14 verses 1 through 10, the prophets urging us and urging the people to use words to return to the Lord: *"O Israel, return to the Lord your God, for you have stumbled because of your iniquity. Take words with you and return to the Lord. Say to him, take away all iniquity, receive us graciously for we will offer the sacrifice of our lips."* That's a powerful passage of the scripture, Hosea.

You see, here's the point: The right words before the court of heaven are very powerful. You see, it's because of our words, that God will forgive us. The sacrifice of our lips and departing from iniquity and returning to the Lord gives the legal right for God to forgive us. That's why John told us to confess our sins in John 1 verse 9. He's talking about the legal right for the forgiveness of sins. He says, *"If we confess our sins, He is faithful and just to forgive us our sins and cleanse us from all unrighteousness."*

Doesn't that make a lot more sense in a legal setting? Our words set legal things in motion. Our words become testimony and agreements with the courts of heaven. Our words grant the Lord the legal right to fulfill his passion for us. And his passion is always mercy and goodness. This is part of what overcomes the accuser or brethren to the word of our testimony.

Again in Revelations chapter 12 verses 10 and 11, it declares that the word of our testimony in agreement with God's purpose overcomes and silences accusation. That verse says, *"Then I heard a loud voice saying in heaven, now salvation and strength and the kingdom of our God and the power of His Christ have come for the accuser of our brethren who accused them before God. Night and day have been cast down and,"* I like this part: *"They overcame him by the blood of the lamb and by the word of their testimony and did not love their lives even unto death."*

Do you see how powerful this is? Part of the word of our testimony is to confess and use words that grant God the legal right to be merciful to us.

The fourth thing for us to come into concert and in agreement with the voices of heaven is our offerings. See, your finances have a voice. Finances are seeds, seeds speak. Words are seeds, words speak. Finances speak, blood speaks, these things speak, they have a continual voice. So, when we bring our finances into the house of God, when we bring it to the altar of God, when we support the work of God, the kingdom of God, with a clean heart and full of passion towards the Lord, these finances add a voice of agreement with heaven.

You know, it's appropriate to offer finances and then prophesy over them in the courts of heaven. When we do, we're becoming a part of the operation of heaven to see his will done on Earth. You see, when you gain a mandate in heaven over your finances, and you begin to declare it in the earth, you're unlocking the power of those finances on Earth. Cornelius was not even a believer; he was a Gentile. But he believed in the God of Israel, he believed in God. And so, the Bible says that his prayers mixed with his alms got the attention of God, where God sent an angel to him and told him what to do. And the angel went and found Peter and told Peter what to do and he brought them together so that the church, the Gentile age, could start. That's us. I thank God for Cornelius every day of my life because I'm not sure we would be here if it was left to some of those disciples.

Number five, we have to resist the devil. If we want to get our prayers answered in heaven, there comes a time to resist the devil. When? Well, once the accuser has been silenced, and the wrestling match in the courts is finished, we are now set to rebuke any demonic forces. This may include the rebuking and renouncing of any or every demonic activity. But, it's incredible how quickly the operation of the devil is stopped and removed once his legal rights are thwarted.

See, once you saw him in the court, it's easy to block him on Earth. But many of us have been praying out of fear: Why do you think that by your much praying, you're heard? It's not your much praying. It's, hey, you don't need to say very much to the devil if you have a legal writ. If God has given you the legal writ, if he's given you the legal jurisdiction, the legal judgment, you don't have to do very much praying.

I mean, I think you should still pray, and sometimes, I think you can pray you're getting the legal jurisdiction. But once you have that, then it's. Excuse me; you're served.

You see, the legal right has been removed, and the rights of his operation are broken. If we have rebuked the devil and it hasn't moved, it's because he still has a legal right to be there. Colossians 3:13 and 14 shows us that Jesus has set in place every legal thing necessary to break satanic strongholds. Look at this. He says, *"And you being dead in your trespasses and the uncircumcision of your flesh, he has made a life together with him."* That's Jesus, *"having forgiven you all trespasses, having wiped out the handwriting of requirements that was against us, which are contrary to us or which were contrary to us, and he has taken it out of the way, having nailed it to the cross."*

So, what is this saying? He's saying, well, every bit of paperwork against us in heaven, Jesus nailed it to the cross and took it out of the way. The words 'handwriting of requirements,' or in some versions 'ordinances,' means a legal document and or law, ordinance or decree. In other words, here's what he's saying. Positionally, Jesus dealt with every accusation, every bit of paperwork that the accuser can use to resist this in the courts of heaven. It's dealt with in the heavenly by Jesus. He did it on the cross. It has been removed, but that doesn't mean that the devil won't try to use it.

Whether it is our sin or the sin of our bloodline, just as you and I had to appropriate what Jesus did for us when we were born again, it wasn't automatic. Just because he died on the cross didn't mean that you were born again. He paid for it in heaven. But there came a time when you have to appropriate it by confessing with your mouth, believing in your heart, and asking Jesus to come into your life. So, it is in the courtrooms of heaven. There are times wherein specifics, and we must appropriate or execute it into place. The devil will seek to use these things against us, but we must take the blood of Jesus and with our repentance, and our faith put what Jesus did for us in that given area. We verbally and with faith and forcibly put into place the work of Jesus on the cross on our behalf. And then when we do this, we have taken away any legal footing that the devil has against us, or that he can try to use.

In fact, in that verse of scripture, the word 'contrary' in these verses means 'covertly.' It says, "Having forgiven you all your trespasses, having wiped out the handwriting of requirements that was against us, which was contrary to us." You can put in there, 'covertly done against us.' They're contrary, but they're done covertly. Sometimes, you don't even know. It's a covert action. The sacrifice of Jesus even deals with the hidden things in our bloodline that are standing against us when by the spirit of revelation, and these bloodline issues come to light. That's why we have 'walking free.' That's why we have 'born to grow.' That's why we have 'breaking the bonds of iniquity.'

But when these issues in your bloodline come to light, you repent of these things, and you apply the blood of Jesus, and you break any place that the devil might have against you, or be trying to exploit. And when we do this, we begin to take charge, or at least, position functionally to get verdicts from the courts of heaven. You see, once we silence the accuser of the brethren, God is free to answer prayers on our behalf. And he does it from a father's heart. He's for you. He's a judge, and he's a Father.

If he talks about the opportunity little, you go before an unjust judge how much more will your Father in heaven judge on your behalf? We have a just judge, and he's your Father. So, when you go, you go boldly, you go confidently. Even when the accuser says you've done this, you've done that, with a broken heart, you say, "Yes, I have. I'm guilty as charged, but the blood of Jesus, my advocate." Do you understand? Any legal place that Satan has been using against us is removed; it's taken away. See, once the legal right is broken, the devil will go where he's resisted.

In James 4, it's very clear: *"Therefore, submit to God. Resist the devil, and he'll flee from me."* Where do we submit to God? In the courtroom of heaven. Once you have a mandate from Jesus, resist the devil, and he'll flee from me. Are you following this? You see, submitting to God involves humility, surrender, repentance, and total submission to the Lord. Once all this is in place, and every replacement of rebellion is totally out of us, all we have to do is resist, and he will flee. The devil no longer has any legal right to stay in our lives. Our rebuke now carries power, and he must flee.

Finally, my last point is, we need to learn how to make decrees. The last thing we do is legal representatives or as legal things have been ordered, is we are free to make decrees. Once we receive the order from the courts, we'll be able to make decrees to carry authority, not only in the courts of heaven but also on Earth. Our decrees are based on what is written in those books. Every objection has been removed, and the judge is now free to fulfill his fatherly position and release his kingdom's will in our lives. Didn't Jesus say it's my father's goodwill to give you the kingdom? He wants to give it to you, but he has to do it legally. He can't just do it. It must be done legally. Does that make sense? See now, nothing is resisting us legally, and our decrees now have power.

To get the full effect of this understanding, I think we need to look at our position in the Bible. The Bible says that we are priests and kings, Revelations chapter 1 verse 6 and Revelations 5 verse 10, it tells us that he has made us be priests. He's made us be kings; priests and kings. Every one of you is a priest and a king. And so, what does this speak of? Well, this speaks of our spiritual positioning in heaven. These are places given to us by and through the work of Jesus Christ on the cross.

The job of a priest is to make intercession, to intercede. The job of a king is to decree things, and they come to pass. When a priest intercedes or when priests intercede, they grant God the legal right to show mercy. This is most clear in the Old Testament, where the high priests, and the priests would go once a year into the throne room of mercy. They would place the blood of a sacrificed bull or of a lamb on the mercy seat. God would then cover the sins of his people and not bring judgment against them. Annually, they had to do this, but God would cover their sins for a year. All the sins that they committed that year, they would be covered so his judgment wouldn't come. It was the day of Passover; the Passover lamb was prescribed by the Lord. And it would give God the legal right to roll the sins of the people back for one more year, the sins of the nation, and the sins of individuals back for another year.

But see, God, by his mandate, needed the function of the priest to administer the blood so that he could grant the legalities that he needed to bless and show mercy. Does that make sense? So, the job of a priest is to intercede strategically so that the legal things are being put in place. Once legal positioning is obtained, then you move into your kingly role. And from that place in the spirit, you can begin to make decrees. This is why we are to be priests and kings to our God.

Now, I think the best place you can see this is in the story that we see in John chapter 11, verses 41 through 44, where Jesus comes to the tomb of Lazarus. Look at what he says, "Then they took away the stone from the place where the dead man was laying, and Jesus lifted his eyes." Listen what he said,

'Father, I thank you that you have heard me, and I know that you always hear me. But because of the people who are standing by, I said this that they may believe that you sent me. Now, when he has said these things, he cried out with a loud voice, Lazarus come forth. And he who had died came out bound hand and foot with graveclothes, and his face was wrapped in cloth. And Jesus said to them, lose him and let him go."

You see, Jesus came to the tomb of Lazarus. And he says to the Father, hey, listen, I know I've already prayed. See, Jesus has already been functioning in this priesthood. He waited four days; he stayed in his priesthood role for four days before even journey to Lazarus' tomb. He has already dealt with every legal reason why Lazarus died prematurely. He has been in the courts of heaven, and he's dealt with the accusations of the devil that allowed Lazarus to die untimely. He knows that legally, everything is in place for what he's about to do. As a result, when he got to Lazarus' tomb, he stepped out of his priestly role into his kingship, and now is no longer interceding; now he has decreed, and with authority, he decrees, "Lazarus come forth."

And I've heard preachers say, if he would have just said 'come forth,' everybody would have come forth. That's not true because he didn't intercede for everybody. He didn't obtain permit for everybody. He obtained a permit in heaven as a priest for Lazarus. The prophets will tell you, 'it's for everybody.' Let me tell you something, some of you will get your healing, and some of you will get your miracles when you go into the courtroom of heaven. When you plead your case, when you've humbled yourself, when you've repented, and a man of God will stand up and say, 'be healed in the name of Jesus.' 'Come forth in the name of Jesus.' 'Rise up,' but a prophet will speak, something will unlock, but it won't be for money, and it won't be a gimmick. It will be the power of God unlocking something from the heavenly for you.

But some of you have gone beyond, and you're beginning to pray for your nation. You're starting to pray for others. Quite frankly, I'd rather see something happen for our nation than happen for me. I'd rather have something happen to the poor people I see on the streets; more and more of them lining up, begging because there's nothing that we're doing for them. God have mercy on us. Can't we unlock something in the heavenly to where wickedness is exposed? Can we unlock something in the heavenly where righteous men, under the blood, rise and take their places, righteous women rise and take their positions? Is it time, isn't there a cause? Are we just gonna keep praying for ourselves, pray for those that we employ, pray for our standing in the world, pray for these elections, that God would remove the filth, and the wickedness and the corruption and the righteous men would find places that they would stand, that somehow, a voice of righteousness would be heard in the land.

What a powerful thing. The Holy Spirit will help us in our weakness to maneuver the courts of heaven. But as we do, we become a part of God's agenda for this planet. Let's move forward and have his kingdom come, and His will be done. Let's move forward and begin to seek what we can do in the heavenly. Bring them the path for our lives, for our families, for our church, for our businesses.

About the Author

Bill Vincent is no stranger to understanding the power of God. Not only has he spent over twenty years as a Minister with a strong prophetic anointing, he is now also an Apostle and Author with Revival Waves of Glory Ministries.

Bill offers a wide range of writings and teachings from deliverance, to experiencing presence of God and developing Apostolic cutting edge Church structure. Drawing on the power of the Holy Spirit through years of experience in Revival and Spiritual Sensitivity. Bill now focuses mainly on pursuing the Presence of God and maintaining Revival.

His books 50 and counting has since helped many people to overcome the spirits and curses of Satan.

Recommended Books

By Bill Vincent
Overcoming Obstacles
Glory: Pursuing God's Presence
Defeating the Demonic Realm
Increasing Your Prophetic Gift
Increase Your Anointing
Keys to Receiving Your Miracle
The Supernatural Realm
Waves of Revival
Increase of Revelation and Restoration
The Resurrection Power of God
Discerning Your Call of God
Apostolic Breakthrough
Glory: Increasing God's Presence
Love is Waiting – Don't Let Love Pass You By
The Healing Power of God
Glory: Expanding God's Presence
Receiving Personal Prophecy
Signs and Wonders
Signs and Wonders Revelations

Web Site:
www.revivalwavesofgloryministries.com

CPSIA information can be obtained
at www.ICGtesting.com
Printed in the USA
LVHW051023190523
747482LV00010B/36/J

9 781794 761251